Inspirational Thoughts

From

Country Living

by
deb darr

ISBN 0-7414-2309-X

Published by:

INFI∞ITY
PUBLISHING.COM

1094 New DeHaven Street, Suite 100
West Conshohocken, PA 19428-2713
Info@buybooksontheweb.com
www.buybooksontheweb.com
Toll-free (877) BUY BOOK
Local Phone (610) 941-9999
Fax (610) 941-9959

Printed in the United States of America

Printed on Recycled Paper

Published January 2005

I would like to dedicate this book to my family---
Without their belief in me I doubt I would have
followed my heart, I love you all.

---Personal Glimpse---

deb was born in the very small town of Lykens, Pennsylvania in 1950. In her early years she lived as a "Service Brat." Her family settled in the Bay Area in California where she attended High School and met and married her High School Sweetheart. Always restless for land and the feel of earth running through her fingers the couple pulled up roots and moved to their present farm home in the Oregon Mountains.

I would like to acknowledge my husband, Greg for all the time he gave proof reading for me. Also, Trinity Lutheran friends who had faith in me and lastly, Glenn Knight, and Jerry Easterly who encouraged me.

TABLE OF CONTENTS

All I Want

All I want is for happiness to be,

The truth unlocks the chains and life is set free.

All I wish is for peace to reign most,

For each one to care, and quiet the boast.

If you understand and feel this way,

It's time for a change, let's face it today.

We can make it right, together we're strong,

If we forge a bound where all can belong.

Stand up, be tall, supporting the just,

Defeating our demons and casting out all lusts.

Turning our hearts towards what we were founded
upon,

As God with us always, together, we're strong.

As Quick as a Wink

Time stands still for no one I heard tell it's true.

As these words sink in the days is almost through.

Instead of being busy chasing after this earth's
schemes,

Stop…take time to look around, and take the time to
dream.

Sit out of doors when the evening is late,

Try to count the stars above, admire what is great.

Leisurely stroll down an uncharted road,

Admire a view, take a casual stroll.

Make the most of you, as life rushes in many different
ways,

Be content for yourself-- and thank the Lord for this
new day.

The Barns

Maybe you've seen them standing all alone

Some are wooden, brick, and some made of stone.

They have stood against the blistering heat of the day,

Time has turned their colors, but most are colored grey.

Some have changed their stature as the earth did shift,

While others never moved, some began to drift.

Please pause to reflect our yesteryear,

If you listen close enough, you'll hear the past so clear.

Of men, machinery, beasts, and townships that were
    new,

These barns reflect of our past and our present too.

Beckoning of the Sea

It calls to me- rolling, splash, gone and return, the sea,

The waves high, strong, unfurling, crashing,

Foaming churning, slapping, deposits to rest what used to be.

Calming, glistening, sparkles, beach combing, easy dream,

Waves lazily roll in and gently move the sand as water trickles to a stream.

With each to dawn a photo can hardly ever capture her,

The pulse of the Sea is restless and if you listen carefully,

She beckons to us come, relax, enjoy, is the steady lure.

Between the Lines

I started reading writing's of hard times and then the
    good,

My mind began to wondering as the writer intended it
    should.

Of carriages, outhouses, woolen clothes and more,

The long cold days of winter, luxuries found at the
    General store.

When reading about days gone by that tested a very
    being,

I found it hard to imagine those days and all those
    scenes.

Started getting lonesome for things that aren't my past,

I'll just live here in the present and let our past

Forever last.

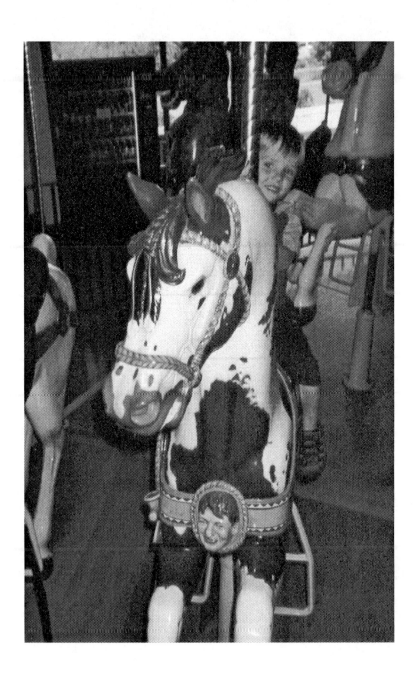

Braden Lee

There is a junior blonde dynamo who's age is almost
  three,

He's here, there, and everywhere, he goes by Braden
  Lee.

Naps are not an option as his busy body moves,

Exploring the world of life is what he's about to prove.

So full of living I wonder if I could have a pint of his
  blood,

Maybe a little transfuse would give life to this old thud.

Entering our world like a hurricane he claimed us and
  he won,

Hey, little guy, we all love you, and THANKS for all
  this fun!!

Buried Treasure

I had begun a task that was long overdue,

Cleaning out brambles of a place we once knew.

This place served as an area for the children to play,

To hide from the scorch of the hottest of days.

Barrels and barrels of years sheddings piled high,

I would ignore the pain, even if my body did cry.

The going seemed endless, long and tiring,

Then my eyes caught a glimpse of something inspiring.

This treasure of yesteryear jolted my mind,

A small dish of play tea set, just one of a kind.

One part of a day that our daughter had shared,

With her imagined playmates and her loved teddy
        bear.

It tugged at my heartstrings, brought tears to my eyes,

I was so taken back, it was quite a surprise.

Her father glancing had sensed what I'd found,

And held me close, with his arms going round.

Tasks they are many, and most quite overdue,

Yet fond memories are precious, as the years carry
        through.

I thank God for the labor of work and good health,

And treasure indeed this discovery of wealth.

Cloudy Days

A shadow filled with gloom, undone.

Caused question in my trust in God,

Leaving me to feel as sod.

Then a glimmer of hope pierced in shreds,

Sending hopes inside of me I thought long dead.

The smallest belief in self came through,

As a mask had covered all that's true.

My creator said, "Believe in Me",

And with belief all shall be free.

Release from want, fear, dread, and doubt,

Sensing what trust was about.

Standing tall as God had planned,

Gone was the dead, arise, new Man.

Comfort Zone

There is a special place that lingers in my memory,

It's a hand made swing suspended from a very old, old tree.

When I needed to get away and sort things out each day,

The swing would seem to set my mood as the world faded away.

As I grew older the swing and I visited less and less,

I thought I had out grown the comfort of the easy sweet caress.

Coming back home as the years hurried passed by,

What was the very first thing that quickly caught my eyes?

The lonely swing was calling sweetly to just me,

Time had come for me to revisit my friend in the tree.

Compassion

Hurriedly, I carried the box of food into the shelter
trying hard not to look at those grieving,

She noticed my haste and said, "Hurry dear, the meal
has been served, the kitchen crew is probably
leaving."

As I passed once again slowing down my pace to focus
on who had spoken,

There sat a young woman with a babe on each side
they smiled as the silence was broken.

As I looked into the eyes I saw love and concern
although their clothes seemed somewhat raggy,

I paused, smiled back, and left them that way, the
weight on my heart seemed heavy and
dragging.

Here was I bringing food to feed people in need,

I wondered was I really trying to quite my greed?

For the Lord did say as you do for others you also do
for me,

On that day he made me who was blind open my heart
to see.

Cowboy

Up before day break alone on the trail,

Facing sun scorchers, whirl winds, snowstorms, and
      hail.

He reins his horse close and rides into the herd,

Sounds of the hooves stirring, he utters no word.

The path is well beaten and worn into the sod,

Down deep to valley his mission well trod.

The day finally over it's the end of the ride,

The events of the day taken well in his stride.

The cowboy hangs up his hat and props up his weary
      feet,

As his day closes down he knows his life can't be beat.

Dedicated to Erma Bombeck

Her advice was acquired from living and it always kept me sane,

The examples she would share with us was true and never vain.

When my "all to serious side" wanted to run and hide,

There she was with her "Tried and True", taken in full stride.

Through the years I thought of her as more than just a friend,

Yet I've never met her, really, only through her pen.

Although she's gone her words still share experience from living,

And I feel she was a person who changed me by her giving.

So with humble over due respect, I Thank you for the lessons,

Lucky was I who read your words, it saved a lot of guessing.

Dew Drops

One night as I lay wide awake while others slept so
sound,

Opening the door bare footed I stepped to feel dew on
the moist ground.

Dampness came to refresh the earth from heat swelters
of the day,

Stepping careful to my special spot, I rest leaving
worries far away.

Moonlight is my beacon while crickets chirped their
songs,

The trek I embarked gently beckoned, "Here's were
you belong."

Sitting quietly down upon the old bench I strained my
eyes to see,

Peace gently removing weights from my heart
allowing life to be.

Needing this place to compose and to rest,

The dew filled night will be a reminder of an adventure
I liked best.

Displacing a Miracle

Our daughter has a flowering plant she's had for many
years,

Although cared for tenderly it's never bloomed,
causing nearly tears.

Then a crisis came to us our faith was near the test,

As days turned into nights each one went without any
rest.

Arriving home with tear dried faces we asked for a
simple sign,

As if froze right in our tracks we witnessed love divine.

A single red bloom brightly swayed open for each of us
to see,

The plant that never bloomed before now blossomed
merrily.

It seemed to say don't despair I've bloomed to show
you God does care,

He knows your hearts, miracles do happen, he has
heard your prayers.

Our spirits lifting we slept that night and thanked God
for his sign,

The prayers were heard the worst had passed, our son
would be just fine.

Do You Know Me?

I have seen you look at me with just a passing glance,

Many seem to understand-I haven't left one chance.

They carefully criticize as they pray to God above,

With the prayers they forget to ask about
      unconditioned love.

When placed before a mirror the blame it isn't theirs,

While viewing my reflection the face is hard to bear.

If awards for stumbling all through life where rated by
      a placing,

The first place cup I would be given for a record most
      disgracing.

Yes, I failed at almost everything,

Made several attempts and now feel the sting.

You see, I've had all the gifts a blessed life really holds,

Casting each one to the wind was acting very bold.

My pages turned to chapters and my book of life is
      gone,

Please look to me with pity Lord, for your gift was
      used for wrong.

Empty Nest

When we started out there was only "Us" two,

Making plans for a family was just what we'd do.

Soon came our first born and happy were we,

Our nest grew to a snug little family of three.

The days filled so quickly hardly time for much more,

The blessings continued and then we were four.

With each rushing week as the activities were abound,

Many days I did wonder if my feet touched the
      ground.

Just as we settled and things started to jive,

No more relaxing...the number was five.

The haze of the days passed quick as a wink,

Just as quick as it started, the numbers did shrink.

In an instant a bedroom, a childhood are all left behind,

The sound of the quiet echoes loud in our minds.

Gradual adjustment to four at the table,

Our family continued as best as was able.

As college approaches we soon felt the signs,

Another is leaving, we knew in our minds.

With three in the home leaving one child to stay,

It didn't take long that he too found his way.

Soon cars, friends, and girls turned his head all too easily,

We accepted these signs as our stomachs turned queasy.

Suddenly it's "Us" back to where we once started,

Getting back into sync, our paths never parted,

The tree grows older, stronger, and a little bit smarter.

Now finding ourselves Grandparents, hey, our family is growing,

With all of the memories, there are more photos for showing.

The coziness settles to our once hectic nest,

Thank you, Lord for allowing this moment of rest.

Faithful Friend

Pitter patter down the hall,

Running fast to fetch the ball.

Strolling down a well worn path,

Chasing cats and dodging baths.

Seems to smile when I feel low,

Wags a tail, accepts a "no."

Years pass quickly as we slow our pace,

The future we aren't afraid to face.

Loving me for what I am.

Thank you, Lord, for my furry friend.

Fall is Coming

Feel the chill that's in the air,

The breeze picks up and tosses your hair.

Stalks of corn sway from side to side,

Orange pumpkins uncovered have lost all pride.

Rakes come out in search of fallen leaves,

Green hoses are stored in sheds or garage eaves.

Lights burn longer with reflections steady,

Fall is coming and I am ready.

Families without Roots

You say you have no Family or relatives that are
    handy?

Let's just put those issues all to rest, for the remedy is
    dandy.

That person you barely know may need a meal or
    maybe just a smile,

Perhaps a brief visit or chat is really just their style.

To share a moment of your busy day,

May bring happiness and chase the sad's away.

We can't pick our family or so I once was told,

So how about adopting people, or would that be too
    bold?

My world shall turn but once around,

I shall gather up my "family" from where no blood
    lines can be found.

Finding Our Place

We came to this place many years ago,

Our dream was for land for a family to grow.

Some people taunted, some friends truly feared

While others mocked, "We'll see you back in a year."

Yet here we are still as happy as could be,

We had no idea what our future would see.

Many long days we kept working and praying,

Thanking the Lord for keeping our spirit from
    swaying.

Now this place is us and we are of this place,

It all came together this land and our space.

Our dream took on meaning, this mountain, our land,

Together with God it turned out oh so grand.

Some tears have been shed, much laughter here, too,

With faith in God and ourselves our dreams have come
    true.

The Flickering Fire Beckons

I so enjoy the glowing of the embers of a fire,

It captures my inner soul, flames release carefree
desires.

To live my life as robust as the steady fire burns long,

Releases me of all pretense, my spineless side stands
strong.

The beckoning of the cozy hearth seems to be all too
inviting,

To stare into the steady blaze is truly most
enlightening.

Reflecting all the yesterdays and feeling no remorse,

Steadily I gaze at the light and plot another course.

Taking the time to calculate embarking a new trail,

Given a chance to plot a path the fire has cast a spell.

Flower Power

We can be touched by the gifts of fresh flowers,

Receiving bouquets have quite magical powers.

An artist creates with much eye catching flair,

We happily accept these to show someone cares.

So if your garden is blessed with a flower or two,

Share the beauty with someone and feel the magic in
you.

For My Ex- Supervisor

You hurt me badly in ways you would not wish to be
     hurt,

Comments about my being, remarks that were curt.

To important ones you seem concerned as wishing to
     gain,

The ones of us less "value" you inflected much pain.

Making crude jokes about me, my work ridiculed,

Yet your position was higher, so why be a fool?

Yes, I'm leaving so I guess you may think that you've
     won,

But really dear "Boss" a new role I've begun.

Unlike yourself I'm not fake or unfair,

I like myself and of others, I care.

As new mornings come I look for life and moments of
     rebirth,

And I can forgive you, oh yes, I can for you are of this
     earth.

Forgiveness

A child grows up feeling less than whole,

Never measuring up to those close by,

Not the best, smartest, brightest, no predetermined
goal.

The years pass and it's still the same.

All the trouble, problems, he's most the blame.

Wasn't named the family name,

Looks different too, such a shame.

Still he finds happiness, loves his God,

Doesn't care if others trod.

His wife, and children love him dear,

The love for family, church, community,

Shows dedication very clear.

Then a call come from family far,

He is needed now, or some of him, anyhow.

Someone is ill, they need his part,

Never mind how they have broken his heart.

NOW he's GOOD enough to be claimed as theirs,

Suddenly he matters...because he'll share.

I have seen him, for him alone...

Family??? They WANT him...

marrow only ..for his bone.

A transplant for a "Brother" foreign,

To save a life he'll give the sovereign.

The man I love and seen mistreated,

By the people he called family,

Mine, to whom they left defeated.

How I can not help but wonder...

If the table was turned back our way,

How important? Would they say,

It's your life...not ours.

Frames

I like to collect moments in time,

The keeping of the memories that help to make it mine.

Loved ones caught and captured from beginning of
      birth,

Happy times and sad ones, to me it's well the worth.

Snapshots of our family farm or a favorite outing,

It's good to sit and share it all even when caught
      pouting.

I frame words to live by when skies sometimes turn to
      gray,

My collections help to bring a smile to get on with the
      day.

Yes, I may have my life in frames it's very plain to see,

But freedom is enclosed in every framework that I see.

Giving

She loved to share with others and that's just what
    she'd do,

It didn't matter what it was, she gave her whole life
    through.

Flowers, Baking, and Casseroles, to brighten someone's
    day,

By sharing these things, part of her was also given
    away.

The then one day a person begged to be passed by,

To this response the giver just turned aside to cry.

Not knowing what she did to hear this request so told,

Giver just decided henceforth not to be so bold.

Others began to wonder what they might have done,

They missed their giver quite a bit along with all the
    fun.

Suddenly it occurred to giver that she still had the right
    give,

And each person has the right to choose on how they
    chose to life.

God Doesn't Exist

Today I watched a child at play,

I sat content to watch this way.

The day was filled with a sky so blue,

Without a single hint of hue.

Wind gusts came on suddenly then completely
    stopped,

I witnessed marching clothes on the line dance flippy-
    flop.

My heart so filled with peace and quiet happiness,

Feeling the gift of love from a baby's tender kiss.

In the distance a hawk was heard to cry,

At that very moment, a butterfly slowly floated by.

After experiencing pleasures in moments such as these,

Who can think to ever doubt that God does not exist?

Grammaw's Lilacs

I stood drinking in the fragrance and slowly closed my
    eyes,

Suddenly drifting back to my youth, I was surprised.

The days were all so sunny with a slight hint of gentle
    breeze,

With each and every visit I did mostly as I pleased.

Sleeping on a fixed-up cot placed in the old screened
    porch,

Mesmerized, I'd stay up late to see the dimming torch.

Grammaw bringing kindness in the form of lemonade,

Sprinkled with her tender love and cookies that she
    made.

Her big old vase stood boldly as it was filled to its
    brim,

As lavender clusters of lilacs fell from cascades of
    within.

Oh, what wonderful scent filled that little room,

Filling every corner with that magic sweet perfume.

Then out would come the photo books, some thicker
    than a leg,

I wanted to see just one more book as I would often
    beg.

Out to her garden she would lead and take my hand
    with pride,

As we cut buckets of lilacs that would not go inside.

We'd gather for neighbors and friends for down the
  street,

Giving arms full of fragrance to those we'd "by
  chance" meet.

Many happy summers I spent in just this way,

As I close my eyes the lilac scent brings Grammaw—

And my youth, of far away.

Grandchildren

Hand prints on windows from looking outside,

Life is an adventure faced with eyes open wide.

Kisses cure hurts from tumbles at play,

Their giggles bring joy to the simplest day.

As they listen to stories engrossed in the tales,

Of riding piggy back on the largest of whales.

Slipping into our hearts our love they have claimed,

From the moment of their birth we're never the same.

Whether it's swinging in air on the count of just three,

"Who's the best Grammaw?"

You guessed it. "It's me!!"

Halloween

It's that time again for the goblins,
As they are getting ready,
The haunting shall be starting soon,
You'll have a trail that's steady.
Coming out when it gets dark they'll
Hope to be quite scary,
You may ask, "Did you wear that costume
Just last year, or was it your sister, Mary?"
For me I'll just enjoy it all and keep those
Treats right handy,
Mercy is needed for the home that isn't
Well supplied with a stock of candy!!!!

Hat Lady

She comes to see me once a week,

This lady of ladies, not at all meek.

Presenting herself with always a change,

By today's standard it seems a bit strange.

Each one matches, each style unique,

Their presence commanding, when the day is so bleak.

Some are feathered while others made of straw,

While on special days they stand very tall.

At first glance you may see yesterday standing very
near,

As for me yes, I see the hats, but also someone dear.

His Cross

I wrapped a cross for Easter and didn't feel the pain,

Never gave a second thought of what I stood to gain.

It was a duty I needed to have done, that and nothing more,

As each shred of cloth was wrapped as I thought not what HE bore.

This prefect lamb who never wronged and did all he was asked,

He didn't argue or complain, and let his own live pass.

Sweet Jesus, how deep your love was and is, you gave up all so I could live,

How much you thought of only me, how you much you had to give.

As I finish wrapping the cross I studied all the shreds,

Guide me Lord to live by you and follow as you've lead.

Asking your forgiveness when I fail to see,

I know you understand it Lord, for I need to forgive me.

Holding Hands

On the spur of a moment have you ever been so bold,

To stretch your arm out purposely and grasp a hand to
hold?

It tells the owner of the hand you care that they are
living,

Your showing for that moment compassion by your
giving.

It only takes a second to share this simple gift,

You both will feel much better in helping to the day a
lift.

I Beat You

While walking with my grandchild he smiled and
    filled with pride,

His little legs jogged far ahead and passing me on my
    left side.

(Un be known to him he beat one of my two speeds,
    slow and slower)

"I beat you, Grammaw", he announced, as we crossed
    the street,

He waited patiently for me, all smiles, expression
    sweet.

I Believe

Sometimes my children think I am a little scary,

Just because they question why I truly believe in
fairies.

The fairies come about to help when my favorite
flowers are crying,

They try to encourage the each bud to grow and keep
on trying.

Whispering their secrets, to give the plants fresh start,

Dusting the ground with fairy dust while singing from
their heart.

Sprinkling glitter on green meadows far away and
distance,

Busily they work all day offering no resistance.

Now I know many folks who believe not as I do,

But I just smile and pass, for my fairy faith is true.

For god can do anything, he's really very wise,

To him it doesn't matter- regardless of the size.

I walk back to nature quickly for the moment is to
seize,

My search is for wee ones, those fairies, which I
believe.

I Like January

It's been a bee's nest all year long,

Early to rise and getting to bed far later than the gong.

Pruning and planting with such tender care,

I couldn't slow down then, it's wouldn't seem fair.

Fun comes with the harvest and canning with the jars,

With rows and rows of "Put Ups" it might appear that
I'm from Mars.

Toss in the whirlwinds we live and face each day,

A rest is really needed lest we go astray.

Then it comes a time to rest and reflect,

To slow down and enjoy the snow on the deck.

With the sipping of coffee and looking outside,

At a world of white beauty God furnishes with pride.

Of catching up on a nap or two,

Reveling in moments instead of "To Do's."

This month is for me, a sweet haven of time,

For renewing, reviewing to make ready for rhymes.

I Look at You

Many people only see a man wearing worn blue jeans,

They miss the kindness in his heart,

Some even think he's rather mean.

The graying of his temples may give a sudden stare,

But let me put you all to rest, this person really cares.

The days are gone of baseballs scores, 4-H,

And soccer fields for chalking,

His voice did boom when games where tied and
        referees were Bauching,

With urgency a new born lamb cried out for his dead
        mom,

The rugged man cradled the babe keeping it safe and
        calm.

Some people will never know the stars that light up in
        the sky,

Yet every time I see him smile stars light inside his
        eyes.

The years have shown the wear that frames the shape

This man I dearly love,

Each night I kneel and thank God for this gift from

Heaven above.

I Want to be Missed

To support and encourage giving large heaps of praise,
Teaching kite flying on crisp windy march days.
Checking for butter with dandelions under a chin,
Falling in love with babies big toothless grin.
Sharing traditions with my daughter in laws,
Witnessing accomplishments by heartfelt applause.
Hugging a child whose hair now shows some gray,
Thanking the Lord for each and every new day.
Tasting the thrill of my first sweethearts kiss,
When God calls for me I just hope I am missed.

I'd Like to be a Hermit

I want to be a hermit, strange as it must seem,

If someone asks much more of me I'll just break down
and scream!!

No, make that more an ogre, with one big scary eye,

So when a person looks at me they will run away and
cry.

I'd like to have things MY way just for a simple day,

No worries and concerns -- where everything melts
away.

Act my age you tell me, do you know how old I AM??

To those words I say to you, take them please, and
scram!

Yes, I admit I'm acting a little less than pure,

I really know the answer, AND I have found a cure.

Silly being grumpy, you know it's not my way,

Guess I'll just get over it and blame it on the day.

The Interview

I'm trying to be perfect -someone whose worth hiring,

As you read my "resume" I hope it seems inspiring.

Questions asked by panels the "one on one" is gone,

I know that the questions are over yet I'll lay awake till dawn.

Chastising myself for answers that seemed absurd and wrong,

Wondering all the while if I prattled on too long.

Suddenly the phone rings telling me I've got the job,

Why didn't I listen to my heart, thinking of all that sleep I robbed?

Next time my soul will rest at peace keeping all that doubt at bay,

If only for a good night's sleep- I'll ask for God's new day.

It Hurts Me

I am sad today when you spoke of disappointment as
   you cried,

Outside my words felt hollow, inside I wished to hide.

The sadness in your story told of hope that fades each
   day,

To trade my place for yours I would, if the pain would
   go away.

We discussed different solutions, decided what to do,

But really, in the long run, the choice it up to you.

Just remember I love you, hoping the future treats you
   mild,

For the heart breaks even harder when the hurt one is
   your child.

Late Lesson

I once thought true happiness was something that was
earned,

Working so hard to achieve this state was a lesson too
late learned.

I've traded off pleasurable moments of childishness
and fun,

No long walks in nature, gone the simple joys as I was
always on the run.

I told myself don't sweat it, someday you'll find the
time,

But suddenly I'm old and gray, my life without a
rhythm.

No matter how much I've earned a rest I cannot find
my ease,

The time grows short for me on earth, while riddled
with disease.

The lesson is a sad one, yes, for I am here to say,

Don't live for tomorrows pleasures,

Live life-- each and every day.

Late Night

Looks like it 's going to be another late night,

As the phone rings we waken with half a fright.

Gratefully you've called to tell us your okay,

However you are calling in at the break of a new day.

As we rush to get our wits and try to get things
straight,

When it comes to finding you, your sleeping in quite
late.

If we cross our fingers and things turn out just right,

You will have a child like you who keeps you up all
night.

Life on the Farm

We aren't the kind of people who work from eight to
   five,

For when we step outside the car our second life comes
   alive.

Many critters beckon to us like they were never fed.

And by the time we've fed them all it's almost time for
   bed.

Our friends think we are crazy for living such a life,

When family comes to see us they think our days have
   strife.

But let us set the score here and tell you how we feel,

Since we choose this style of life we know that it's a
   deal.

So please don't worry about us as our duties may seem
   soaring,

Now that we are farmers our life is never boring.

The Lone Cow Hand

He works driving cattle against the greatest of odds,

Wore well to his work pushing on through snow plods.

When all earth is nestled and snugly tucked inside
their bed,

The cowpoke pushes forward hoping there's nothing
to dread.

Shaking icicles from a kerchief tied over his face,

He's been here before and he knows his place.

The herd is his life and to it he belongs,

Arriving on time dedication is strong.

Around the next bend the morning is breaking,

He'll move cattle to safety with a body that's aching.

His mission accomplished, the herd's safe and sound,

Our cowhand rides chasing sun up -- coffee's just the
next town.

Look for Beauty

I want to hold a hummingbird close inside my hand,

I'd like to follow a rainbow to see it touch the land.

To really be small enough to watch the fairies play,

Listening to the wind understanding what she has to
    say.

Riding on a snowflake before it comes to rest,

A first row seat to see the sun arriving with full zest.

Watching a new flower as each petal opens wide,

Viewing a shell cast from the sea looking deep inside.

God means for us to see these things that he sends our
    way,

I thank you Lord for the little things,

The beauty in each new day.

Love

This man of mine I married he is my truest friend,

This man of mine I married will be mine until the end.

This man of mine I married shares my every thought,

This man of mine I married knows just how much I've
bought.

This man of mine I married eats everything I cook,

This man of mine I married has a strong yet gentle
touch,

This man of mine I married is loved so very much.

This man of mine I married will always make me smile,

This man of mine I married I'll keep him for awhile.

Madilynn Iris

Little wee one I hold so near,

You are a gift we cherish dear.

Those big blue eyes and coal black hair,

I'd know those ankles anyway.

Looking up at me I whisper a silent prayer,

Please god watch over us both, and the bond we share.

To our grandchild "Welcome" with a happy heart,

We've loved you from the very start.

Magic Moments

While going through old clothes of ski things we once
used,

I came across a snowsuit, smiling, I began to muse.

The worn out old apparel was some what left in sheds,

But visible seen was a fleeced hood brightly trimmed in
red.

Both legs zipped easily from toes to top of the head
with ease,

To keep a little body warm to block out the cold breeze.

The clad wearer resembled a small little red bug,

If the weather was chilly the child would be kept snug.

As the snow filled the day those cherub cheeks would
glow,

Along with the rosy red nose of this babe peeked out
for such a show.

If I close my eyes tight I still see the glee,

Of my children in snow play, as they dodge a big fir
tree.

Dear Lord, stop the time clock for me to cradle all this
bliss,

For there isn't the smallest moment I would care to
miss.

As dark turned to dawn and the daybreak turned to
light,

I want to keep all of these visions tucked away framing
       each just right.

Fast forward those yesterdays to now our grown up
       kids,

Busy now with their lives and trying to make things fit.

Help us all to enjoy the little happiness that we find
       along our way,

So all we need is to close our eyes keeping the treasures
       here to stay.

Memory Captured

One day long ago on a fine spring day,

I witnessed the beauty of a child at play.

The wind's gusts ushered in a crisp cool breeze,

Allowing air borne kites to climb with incredible ease.

On the distance a small child and her kite danced
merrily along,

While accompanied by a horse full of grace, so sure
and strong.

As the horse trotted along the child seemed as happy
as she,

Together they darted, swooped, and circled, the
dancers made three.

I watched, oh so carefully as not be become an
intrusion,

Asking myself "Could this really be just be an
illusion?"

The recaptured memory vividly recalled while
traveling the same old trail,

Eyes that jolted open cautiously read, "One Family
horse for sale."

NO!! NO!! screamed my brain not this one, so rare,

Would I over step my bounds to mention I cared?

To speak of the joy and wonder displayed,

I'll tell what I saw on that windy spring day,

Of child, kite, and creature together at play.

My questions were answered yes, we must say it's true,

The child grown now in college, is torn with what to do.

Funding was needed, a change seemed to be best,

The horse deserved more, still showing her zest.

But what of the friend, the silent watcher who would rather just stay,

Whose understanding and devotion weathered out each passing day?

While telling my story the family thought back to the past,

Didn't it just make sense to keep a horse whose loyalty would last?

For their future days of grandchildren should experience this rite,

With happiness that comes with a horse, a child, and a kite.

Monday Mornings

Another busy morning of rushing out the door,

Haven't a clue how I'll manage as I spill coffee on the floor.

Hey, What's that I've stepped in? A "gift" from someone's dog,

No use now to hurry, the morning's filled with fog.

Please, NO!! Mr. log truck, I took great pride in my car wash,

Geez, *thanks* a heap my window now resembles mucky slosh.

Here it is! My place of work just over the horizon,

I've been there for who knows how long, and this I'm not a-lyin'.

It could be worse oh yes it could, I should an aloner,

Laughing at myself all week long for being such a groaner.

Here comes Friday my favorite day, it wasn't all that bleak,

That's what I'll say this whole weekend until I start next week.

My Garden

Come visit my garden is what my sign reads,

Mixed in with the flowers you'll also find weeds.

Potatoes keep growing that were long ago planted,

As I walk I see beauty sometimes taken for granted.

Between lavender lilacs and honeysuckle I smell the
sweet earth,

The hours I have toiled brings me happiness and a
sense of worth.

Each year I look forward to planting seedlings anew,

With joy I prepare seed beds knowing just what I'll do.

Strolling among the hollyhocks and herbs the sound of
silence abounds,

While I drink in the pleasures of planting in ground.

Photo by Nancy Kurz.

My Jenny

She stands silently letting me think I have the bigger
    brain,

Patiently she watches as I feed her hay and grain.

Waiting for me to leave an unlatched gate loose and
    hanging free,

Then out she trots to leave me guessing, "Where the
    heck is she? "

I find her and lead her back as I watch her through the
    day,

Those big brown eyes look right at me, teasing, in her
    gentle way.

I know secretly she likes this game for which I am the
    pun,

To her it's just another day of having donkey fun.

My List

I felt so totally organized,
Staying up late that night,
To write down all my errands,
Just to get things right.
No doubling back would do for me,
Or driving criss-cross downtown.
Too many trips I'd spun my wheels,
Forgetting most of what I came for,
Turning a good time upside down.
I was ready. Set and good to go,
The skills now mine just thrilled me so.
Eyeglasses, checkbook, and keys in fist,
Good grief…I just misplaced my list!!!

Neighbor

I often ask myself, "What is a good neighbor?"

Is it a person who takes the time to give a hand in
    labor?

Or a person who lifts you up when you're feeling low,

Sometimes you might be surprised when they tell you
    where to go.

When a person puts them self in your shoes for a day,

And they still treat you kind, even if things aren't
    going their way.

I hope the type of neighbor for everyone to see,

Is that special neighbor that I would want to be.

Neskowin

We first searched to find the sea, found her and
Felt to this place a belonging,
Our travels always led back to this spot,
There wasn't a doubt, the calling was strong.
Many years of one day visits this place called to us,
We lost all resistance.
Watch the waves, explore the shore,
The Sea awaiting evermore.
Trust this place and call me home,
Never worry, no more shall you roam.
Rest a bit drink in the breeze,
Never change, do as you please.
God knew our hearts, we weren't forsaken,
Into our souls a bond was in the making.
This part of peace and shelter true,
Tranquility surrounds us the long days through.
Every visit I thank God again,
For feelings of home with a dear old friend.

No More Excuses

I would of done that BUT....

I could of done that IF ONLY...

I should of liked to have been HOWEVER....

Our life slips away from us before

We are ready to realize our fullness.

Do the things that really matter today,

Give a little extra of yourself,

Brighten someone's sky that seems to have gone away.

Count for something worthwhile,

Add a little merriment, just by sharing a smile.

The peace of knowing your presence made a
    difference,

Shall be a light to a person who might have inner strife

It will strengthen your bond to humans and add a
    bonus to your life.

Nothing is Forever

Nothing is forever, it really seems a shame,

Why do things have to change, and who is it I can
blame?

Just when life seems to fit just right it up and get's the
nerve,

For turning everything all around and throwing in a
curve.

For me I like everything to feel comfortable, like
breathing in and breathing out,

Then change comes in and spoils it all, just makes me
want to shout.

My favorite garden store is selling, moving and going
away,

What I really wanted most is for them to forever stay.

Getting used to something new is such a pain to me,

Why, oh why I ask myself does change come so
frequently?

I guess there's nothing I can do but lift these dragging
feet,

Accept what's new...oh what the heck, I admit it, I am
beat.

Old Homestead

For awhile I drove by you everyday,

Yellow fading paint holds on while aging into the gray.

Windows missing like falling teeth,

Your foundation crumbles exposing sod beneath.

Oh, what a beauty you once were,

The family gathering place for sure.

The babes slept under the old shade tree,

While summer wheat fields waved tall and free.

A wrap around porch for sitting a spell,

The resting place for tired, and those for whom wished
well.

The plaque est. 1893 can be read on your old south
side,

Graceful rusted gate left standing swung open wide.

I nod at you as I pass you by,

Deep within my soul I think I want to cry.

Whispering a prayer for someone to uncover,

The majestic place that stands alone awaiting
rediscover.

Our Hunter Riley

Dear little boy with the beauty smile,

Please stay little for a time so we can hold on for a
while.

You cute sayings are straight "Off the Cuff,"

And of those sweet little dimples were can't get
enough.

The world is all yours to discover and claim,

Each day is a journey and you share it's fame.

Who can resist those curls on the top of your head?

Making it a challenge when it's time for your bed.

A helper you are and right from your start,

You are a "Hunter" -- for you captured our hearts.

Our Soldier

He served his country and gave her part of his life,

Leaving his only family, one small son and a wife.

Now his son is grown with family small,

Son now serves his country, standing very tall.

How many lives will it take,

To save our nation from the brink of break?

Our history must be preserved our people must stand
    bold,

Their guard is keeping strong so we should never fold.

Please honor the ones who serve us true,

Always fly high our Red, White, and Blue.

Play Ball
(for my son's, and their father)

He tries to have patience for the late afternoon,

Getting himself ready for the game starting soon.

He lives for the special night every week,

And rallies his best so his team won't get beat.

He loves each position and plays them all well,

Yet he never brags himself up, his head doesn't swell.

It's being a part of the team that brings him alive,

A job well done in the end is all he will strive.

It all comes together with the swing of the bat,

With rounding each base he's knows where he's at.

This player of baseball, the season goes on,

And thankful is he that it's lasted so long.

A Place of Solace

In the world we live in we are busy evermore,

Each of us need a space where we can close the door.

Away from all the demands when perfect isn't enough,

We seek a piece of quiet when the goings get too
rough.

Find that little haven where you may have "Time Out,"

To listen to your inner self, discover what your all
about.

You have to PROMISE to leave guilt at the front door,

Find the gifts of simpleness and all the beauty that's in
store.

Now you can step back refreshed, you'll find you
haven't lost your place,

Life will have new meaning as you rejoin the human
race.

Ranch Hand

All he has is his horse and the range,

For him it's enough, thought other's think him strange.

The call to his duty runs deep to the mark,

Working from sun up till long after dark.

Once asked if he'd have it any other way,

His smile came on slowly and he just didn't say.

For some things mean more than what's tucked safe
and tight,

And so it is for the Cowboy who rides away in the
night.

Rebel

He started out with big blue eyes and a smile a mile
long,

While playing in his childhood games he always had a
song.

Standing for the things he believed, going against the
grain,

Many times his eyes and voice portrayed his sadness
and his pain.

Accepted things about himself hoping others would,

Wishing at times he could conform yet asking himself
if he could.

Standing on his own and while needing others so,

Growing up on his own terms he forged many years
ago.

His path is far from easy as he stands to find his way,

Our wish for you dear son is for happiness and love to
fill your days.

A Roofer

Perched way up on top where few wish to be,

Sits one single man armed with great dignity.

He labors long hours through sun scorching days,

Exposing his body to those ultra bright rays.

Little think of him or that he might have a brain,

None really do care if he hurts or he's strained.

If a roof has a leak he's king of the hill,

They seem very pleased till it's time for the bill.

He isn't a stranger to trig, and calculus is his friend,

While figuring square footage the tape has no end.

So this person is a man with so little to gain?

Hey, let me see you climb any height in the wind and
     the rain!

Rural Child

Barefoot bicyclist peddles by,

Not a care in of worry showing,

Face smiling, head turned towards the sky.

As the wind blows leaves around the earth,

I caught a passing glimpse of beauty in youthful mirth.

Dressed in denim and caring not,

Burning sunlight my way you pass,

The child within eager to share your plot.

While city limits quicken their pace,

Country whispers her gentle hush, letting the quite
　　　beauty set the pace.

Ride away my little rural child,

Stay as you are-- don't change,

Ride towards a land where dreams grow wild.

Scarecrow

I like to visit with you each and every fall,

Your fashion rarely changes, sometimes your short or tall.

A smile always dons your face even when skies are gray,

Some days you do little more than chase the blues away.

When I see the character that was formed by your master's hand,

Maybe being just a "Scarecrow" is something rather grand.

Selfish Me

Some days I do wonder why I got out of bed,

As the day comes unraveled I feel a sense of dread.

Then something awakens from deep in my soul,

I'm gently reminded of whose in control.

Do have more than many others have had?

Am I still free to roam over all lands?

If I'm feeling weary rest is easy to find,

Shelter is home, the place where I can speak my mind.

Taking a deep breath I feel humble and free,

Thanking My Lord for the blessing from he.

I know I'm lucky...God gives all and more than I need,

He can't possibly keep up with my greeds.

Serenity Jade

The word serenity brings a tranquil thought to mind,

Yet when I encounter you, peace is hard to find.

Those busy little fingers are missioned to explore,

Opening and rooting through each and every drawer.

Scurrying on those baby feet a quick food stop of
    refueling,

I watch you rub a sleepy eye, but know you are just
    fooling.

Life is an adventure, with surprises to explore,

And when you visit Grandma, love starts at the front
    door.

Silent Monster

It can enter our lives as quietly as a mouse,

Then change everything, life, bringing fear inside our
house.

Patterns of routine for the everyday family,

Drawing closer together to avoid this calamity.

Shock, disbelief, then mountains of tears,

Silently The Monster robs it's victim of years.

Each night and each day my prayers are quite steady,

Asking for healing. The Father's touch...this person's
isn't ready.

Where is the fairness, never finding an answer,

For someone diagnosed with inoperable cancer.

The future unsteady the path seems to twist,

With the stakes so high Monster release...they'll be
missed.

Pain enters my soul, I'll surrender this grief,

Hold fast to convictions, religion, belief.

Answers aren't coming and God holds the key,

But I can't help but wonder why this has to be.

Slow Me Down Lord

Some days feeling like I leapt from bed in a full run,

Rushing to demanding days exhausted and undone.

Most of the "important" things could wait a week or two,

Moving the agenda page checking off my list "TO DO."

I know that I am blessed by you to have a busy life,

Yet too many lists of "Honey Do's" can only lead to strife.

Slow me down Lord, talk to me and put me in my place,

Shake me if you need to, for life is not a race.

I need to linger over spoken words that fall upon my ear,

Casual moments of reprieve, to rejoice that I am here.

Help see the issues for others that are real,

Focus me on daily needs of how my brothers feel.

Gentle times are waiting for all God has in store,

All I need do is pace myself before I reach the door.

Small Town

I love being of a small town,

A person can't get lost in it,

One has time to talk, walk, stop and look around.

Neighbors know each other and share each other's life,

People pull together, with small victories- each other's
strife.

The unwritten rules are hard and fast,

Most everything is closed on Sundays,

We take time to make joy last.

Vendors plants for sale are safe staying out all night,

Yard sales are over by five or dusk,

Everyone has a sense for what is wrong or right.

The children are "looked after" with everyone's
parental eyes,

Respect is taught at an early age with priorities very
high.

You may wonder where my heart shall be forever
found?

The plain and simple truth of it is here,

Right here, in this small town.

Snow Magic

The snowfall was deeper than ever before,

As the flakes fell covering most the front door.

Our children were "Charged" for they knew in their heart,

School would be canceled- It just wouldn't start.

The mountain we live on is elevated high,

When snow drops for us it nearly touches the sky.

So Father Darr stayed home serving as shuttle was he,

Depositing youngsters to share the fun and the glee.

Snow forts and tunnels were constructed all day,

Laughter and fun could be witnessed at play.

Inside our old wood stove roared as it heated and dried,

Warming hats, boots, and mittens that were draped a mile high.

Kids inhaled hot cocoa and gobbled up sandwiches as quick as a wink,

As they dashed for the door dirty dishes were tossed in the sink.

As evening approached we were put to the test,

Could they ALL spend the night? For night snow play was best.

When bedtime had settled every blanket was busy,

While surveying the sight I almost got dizzy.

As I now reflect upon the magic snowfall came to
   bring,
The joy of that day was sent to us by angels on wings.

A Special Day

It was my birthday, my own special day,

But I felt all alone and the sky seemed so gray.

Contemplating chores I just couldn't start,

Feeling so lonely it hurt in my heart.

Took a walk to the mailbox, maybe someone did care,

As I approached I hesitated, with eyes fixed into a
stare.

Resting ever so gentle at the base of the post,

Was a beautiful birds nest as if placed by a ghost.

Glancing quickly to see, could someone have guessed?

A treasure from nature the things I love best.

Marveling, I turned home with a new bounce in my
gate,

I knew I WAS special, I KNEW I did rate.

God who knows all thank you for sharing,

Your gift was just right, your message of caring.

I wondered how God knew just what it would take,

For me to realize I had made a mistake.

Each day is a blessing sent from him above,

It's my turn to reflect...the gift of his love.

To Our McKenzie Rose

You entered our life as our "number one,"
And from that moment our new role had begun.

Now watching you grow before all of our eyes,

Each year is a blessing and filled with surprise.

More than a grandchild, to us you belong,

Adding your roots our family tree grows strong.

With each new year of life that comes unto to you,

Please keep God in your heart in all that you do.

Happy Birthday, our dear one, it's your special day,

Our wish for you blessings, that always will stay.

Took a Time Out

I took a "Time Out" a time just for me,

I was overdo to this most would agree.

Catching up on all those outstanding projects,

With no interruptions seemed really quite the logic.

The first day or so the candle burned long,

Sleep was delayed oh yes, I was strong.

"Have a good time", my loved ones all teased,

I was the Queen, I did as I pleased.

Suddenly it hit me, reality came down,

Being rather self centered my smile now donned a
    frown.

I NEEDED these people, to them I belong,

A project is fine, when they are along.

Never again will I want it totally just MY way,

Close to my loved ones is where I plan to stay.

Touch Stone

I want to be a touch stone, someone whose hand to
    hold,

When burdens need to be lifted, when the world seems
    dark and cold.

To brighten someone's sadness, to share a smile or two,

For God has been MY touch stone - he's always pulled
    me through.

Turning of the Page

Recently I've noticed many things that have changed,

Just one look in the mirror-I'm seeing someone strange.

The wheels of life are turning in a different way,

Causing me to wonder, what's important for this day.

Many things taken for granted, the starry nights so
    true,

Noticing more the precious things like the sky a perfect
    blue.

The gathering of loved ones, sharing all we can,

Now it all seems crystal clear this is my Lord's plan.

Slowing down just a bit to enjoy all GOD has given,

Accepting things I cannot change, reasons to keep
    living.

Taking time for simple things I think it comes with age,

God knew it all, he set me straight,

It's time to turn the page.

Photo by Nancy Kurz.

Visit Our Farm

Come please and visit our farm,
The animals and life are friendly,
Each has its own personality,
None will do you any harm.
Each day starts out with a list to do,
Many chores carry over but we manage to get through.
Some times the only sound heard is the song of a bird,
Many feelings enter the soul without any word.
The view may vary depending on where you stand,
Let me quite convince you that every view is grand.
As dusk settles in your weary bones may tire,
Yet given any choice at all our farm is my desire.

A Walk in the Woods

I love to walk into the woods especially in the fall,

As sunlight filters through the trees I'm awed and feel
so small.

Stillness helps me to relax and feel the tranquil bliss,

It would be a pity not to see this sight, realizing what
I'd miss.

Shades of green, gold, orange, and red blend with each
new trail,

Ferns, moss, fir needles, and broken branches remind
me life is frail.

A bird's discarded feather rests softly on the land,

Refreshed, I leave my woods letting go of nature's
hand.

Walking With My Father

I was having trouble sleeping, tossing to and fro,

Puzzled by the questions of why God's let things go.

Suddenly I awoke a vision before my eyes,

Scared at first then I saw something materialize.

An unclear form stood very close and gently took my hand,

In a flash viewing earth and every person--while floating above the land.

From the a haze that surrounded me there was a question to be asked,

Requests are made and said by those who rarely have a task.

"You feel I have given up yet you don't understand,

Things that go on today are a far cry from God's plan."

"Many times my heart is saddened because so many turn away,

No one wants to turn to me, of the earth they wish to stay."

"Please Father, God, I know it is of me you speak,

I want to trust and keep the faith, I guess I'm pretty weak."'

"Use me Lord, to be your tool to help others with their doubt,

Trusting you each and every day is what I'll be about."'

"Rest now child," he spoke leaving me to wake and
show his way,

That is how I'll hope to live my faith from now till all
my days.

Welcome Home

My home is filled with things some folks would just
   throw away.

Clutter collecting are scattered here, there, and every
   other way.

But memories abound both inside and outdoors,

Trees plants just as saplings are twenty feet or more.

The easy coziness and comforts of each familiar sight,

Makes coming home special and a place that seems
   quite right.

What is Happiness??

Do you achieve happiness from having great health?

Or is really found by acquired wealth?

What about your job you struggled so hard land?

No one really guessed about the tricks you had at hand.

I guess happiness can be the things mentioned up above,

But what are they REALLY, without the element of love?

Where is Justice?

Where is justice you may ask,

Seems to me justice is a thing of the past.

For some breaking laws to them is no "Big deal",

Their acts leave scars upon our souls to never
completely heal.

Punishment is served and carried out by we the
victims,

Real life crimes acquired while watching all those
sitcoms.

Forgive them for what they have done,

Tried and freed to harm again, all for reckless fun.

It's time to turn our system around,

Wrong isn't Right, but can Right be found?

Please Lord, help me not to hate or feel cruel,

I want to obey and keep the "Golden Rule."

When earth life is over and I cross the gate,

Shall justice prevail- or will victims still wait?

Who Will Tend My Flowers

I love all my flowers as most everyone knows,

I wonder who will tend to them when it's my time to
go?

Will they strong enough to grow on their own,

Or shall they wither and die never to be resown?

Wishing pleasure being brought to others has it has
me,

Please clear their path of weeds so they grow so
splendidly.

I wish for someone to care and see my plants as I do,

Then I shall rest ever at peace, my work will carry
through.

Yard Sale

I went to your yard sale the other day.

You were missing...you had passed away.

The treasures you held dearly here on earth,

Were all being sold...for what they were worth.

Family members gathered from far and from near,

They sold your gift picture that read, "Mother Dear."

It was hard to say what should go or what should stay.

Many memories were sold on that rainy Fall day.

Someday the tables will turn, shall they cry or maybe
    weep,

Selling treasures to others to use and to keep.

Forgive us Dear Lord for want of the material things,

Our home can't come with us, nor our diamonds or
    rings.

Be gentle to loved ones, to us please be kind,

When the yard sales have ended bring us peace of
    mind.

You Won't Know Until You've Tried

"You won't know till you've tried," my old aunt used
to say,

And like her and those words oh how I wished them
fast away.

So often had I heard that phrase when asked to do a
chore,

Or any other duty I just knew would turn a bore.

As years passed on before me as if burned into my
soul,

It took much work and effort to keep my self control.

Never realizing this was a mentor when only just a
child,

Now there she stood smiling back at me her manner
really mild.

Her life had many troubles and heartbreaks that's for
sure,

But she took it all and stood her ground that saying
was her cure.

Now as my own babe rejects my advice and rolls her
eyes heaven bound,

I smile while the vision crosses my mind to help me
stand my ground.

I turn to face this cherub, and whisper in my stride,

How can you know just how you'll do?

"You won't know until you've tried."